selections from

Open
House

Solo Piano Compositions and Arrangements
by Lorie Line

Edited by Anita Ruth

©1997 Lorie Line Music, Inc.
222 Minnetonka Avenue South
Wayzata, MN 55391 (952) 474-1000

Notes From The Artist

'They say home is where the heart is. I know it's always been true for me. My home is where so many of my feelings are centered. It's where I'm most comfortable. It's where I do my best work. So this time around, I decided to do an album right in my own home on my own piano. All the music in this book was created here. And the photos were taken here, too.

At the time I was writing and arranging this music, my family was spending our first days in the dream home we always wanted to build. Through its windows, I was able to watch three beautiful seasons change while I wrote and arranged this music. It was an inspiring sight, and my feelings at the time are now a permanent part of this book.

Included in this book are a variety of styles which I hope you'll enjoy… Celtic, traditional, and two new originals.

This is the music I'd play for you if you were a guest in my home. I hope you'll enjoy it and have the occasion to share it with others in your own home."

Lorie Line

About the Originals

Jackson's Girl -When I first played this song for my 3-year-old son, Jackson, it was untitled. We were on our way home riding in my car. He was *really* listening (he loves drums). He turned and looked straight at me and said, "Mom, I'm riding with you 'cause you're my girl." He is going to know the perfect thing to say to a woman.

Forest Lake -Named after a very special place to me, this song was written as the ice moaned and I anticipated seeing the lake open and life to begin again.

Full orchestrations of all Lorie Line music are available by special order for schools, churches, and ensembles. Call 1-800-801-5463 (LINE) for more information.

Table of Contents

Jackson's Girl

Lorie Line and
Kenni Holmen
Arranged by Lorie Line

Innocently

With passion

8

Boldly

The Ash Grove

traditional Welsh

Simply

Arranged by Lorie Line

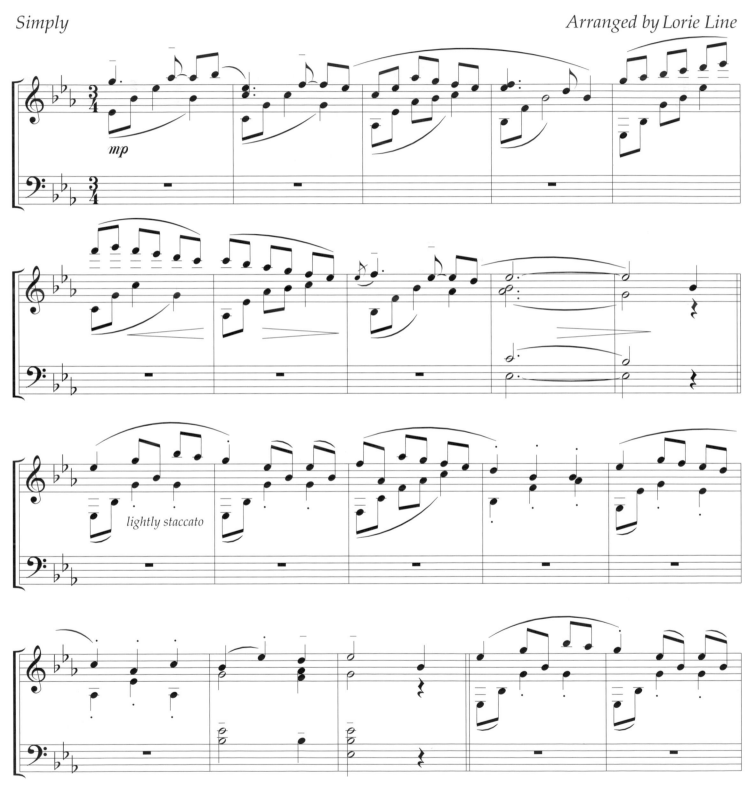

Delicately

A little faster

A Tempo

With a confident manner

A little faster

A Tempo

Star of the County Down

traditional Irish

Soulfully

Arranged by Lorie Line

decrescendo   poco   a   poco

8va

(Both staves 8 va)

L.H. over

p

(8va)

(8va)

Sidh Beag and Sidh Mor

traditional Irish

Stately

Arranged by Lorie Line

*Roll up slowly,
imitating the drone
of the bagpipe.*

Quietly, flowing

Forest Lake

Rubato, in a reflective manner

Lorie Line

As at the beginning

Child-like

As at the beginning

ritard

The Rights of Man

traditional Irish

Quickly, with spirit

Arranged by Lorie Line

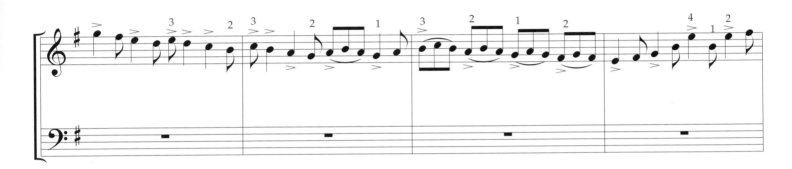

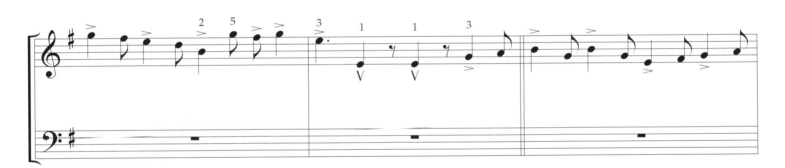

(Roll up)

8vb _ _ _ _ _ _ _ _ _

A Tempo

Molto Ritard

The Lord's Prayer

traditional hymn

Reverently

Arranged by Lorie Line

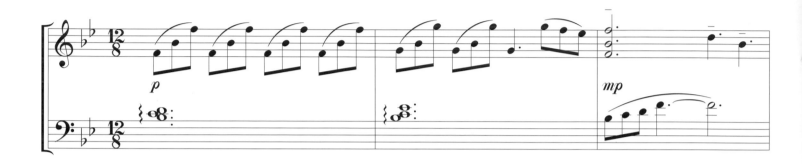

With quiet strength

crescendo   poco   a   poco